Bible Study Series
for junior high/middle school

THE TRUTH ABOUT BEING A
Christian

Loveland, Colorado

The Truth About Being a Christian
Core Belief Bible Study Series

Credits
Editors: Lisa Baba Lauffer and Karl Leuthauser
Managing Editor: Michael D. Warden
Chief Creative Officer: Joani Schultz
Copy Editor: Janis Sampson
Art Director: Lisa Chandler
Cover Art Director: Helen H. Lannis
Cover Designer/Assistant Art Director: Bill Fisher
Computer Graphic Artist: Ray Tollison
Photographer: Craig DeMartino
Production Manager: Gingar Kunkel

Unless otherwise noted, Scriptures quoted from The Youth Bible, New Century Version, copyright © 1991 by Word Publishing, Dallas, Texas 75039. Used by permission.

ISBN 0-7644-0859-3

10 9 8 7 6 5 4 3   06 05 04 03 02 01 00 99

Printed in the United States of America.
Visit our Web site: www.grouppublishing.com

Bible Study Series
for junior high/middle school

contents:

the Core Belief: ▼ Salvation

It's a basic tenet of Christianity. Without it, we can have no relationship with God because he is holy and we are sinful. But by his grace, he freely offers us a gift—his holy Son as the sacrifice for our sin. Jesus Christ laid down his life and rose up from the grave so that we can live forever.

As students participate in the studies under this Core Christian Belief, they will discover that salvation can be theirs if they believe in Jesus Christ, turn away from their sin, and have faith that Jesus has their present circumstances and their eternal well-being in his hands. Jesus redeems all of us—freeing us *from* the power of sin and death *to* new life in Jesus Christ.

the ▼ Helpful Stuff

SALVATION AS A CORE CHRISTIAN BELIEF
(Or How to Get a Clean Slate)

7

ABOUT CORE BELIEF BIBLE STUDY SERIES
(Or How to Move Mountains in One Hour or Less)

10

WHY ACTIVE AND INTERACTIVE LEARNING WORKS WITH TEENAGERS
(Or How to Keep Your Kids Awake)

57

YOUR EVALUATION
(Or How You Can Edit Our Stuff Without Getting Paid)

63

the ▼Studies

Parents Are People Too 15

THE ISSUE: Parents
THE BIBLE CONNECTION: Romans 3:21-26; 5:12-21; and 6:5-14, 20-23
THE POINT: We all need new life in Christ.

Stairways to Heaven? 25

THE ISSUE: Eternal Life
THE BIBLE CONNECTION: Mark 10:17-27; John 14:6; 17:1-3; and Ephesians 2:4-9
THE POINT: Faith in Jesus is the only way to eternal life.

A Technicality in the Law 35

THE ISSUE: Grace
THE BIBLE CONNECTION: Genesis 1:26-31; 3:1-24; Exodus 20:1-17; Psalm 139:13-16; Isaiah 55:8-9; Matthew 22:34-40; John 3:14-21; Romans 3:10-18, 23; 6:22-23; 8:1-6; Ephesians 2:8; and James 2:10
THE POINT: Life is empty without Jesus.

Rock Solid 47

THE ISSUE: Faith
THE BIBLE CONNECTION: Leviticus 11:45; Judges 6:11-24, 33-40; 7:1-22; 2 Samuel 22:2-3; Proverbs 3:5-6; Acts 17:24-25; Hebrews 11:1; and 1 John 4:7-10
THE POINT: You can trust God.

▼Salvation as a Core Christian Belief

The goal of nearly every religion is for its followers to have a joyous afterlife. In most religions that means hard work and suffering during life on earth as followers strive to attain a level of spirituality that assures their "salvation." However, God tells us that we must be perfect to live with him in heaven. And there's no way we can attain perfection on our own. No matter how hard we try to be good, we'll always fall short of God's perfect standard. That leaves us destined for an eternity of separation from God.

That's where the good news of God's salvation comes in! God loves us so much that long before any of us turned to him, he gave his own Son to suffer and die an agonizing death so that our sins could be forgiven. Then Jesus rose from the dead, defeating death for us so that we can live eternally with him—starting on the day we ask forgiveness for our sins and trust Jesus with our lives.

But do your kids know and live by this good news? In today's culture, your young people have exposure to all kinds of religions proclaiming different works that will gain them salvation—praying five times a day, meditating for hours, or cleansing themselves in a river. Our performance-oriented society further seduces them into thinking they must do good works to be saved. Other young people don't even know they're lost. The "I'm OK, You're OK" mentality blinds them from their deepest need.

In *The Truth About Being a Christian*, your students will have the opportunity to uncover the folly of these false philosophies and theologies by looking at the reality of salvation through Jesus Christ. In the first study, kids will be challenged with the fact that we *all* need new life in Jesus. They'll be encouraged to extend mercy to others in need of Jesus' changing power including their **parents.**

In the second study, kids can learn that they can't work their way to heaven or find salvation through false religions. They can discover that faith in Jesus is the *only* way to **eternal life.** They'll be encouraged to put their faith in Jesus and will be reminded of the assurance of his promises.

In the third study, kids will have the opportunity to discover the impact that salvation can have on their immediate lives. As they investigate the abundance of God's **grace,** they can see that life is as empty without Jesus as it is purposeful and fulfilled with him.

In the final study, students will examine their own **faith** in God. By looking at God's solid character, they can learn that God is absolutely trustworthy. They can see that God is their immediate and eternal salvation, and they can completely trust him with their lives.

Most people who accept God's gift of eternal life do so before they turn twenty, so the teenage years are vitally important in your kids' lives. Finding God's salvation now will not only empower your young people to live powerful, productive lives for God, it will also prevent them from wasting years in which they could've known a God who loves them more than life.

For a more comprehensive look at this Core Christian Belief, read Group's **Get Real: Making Core Christian Beliefs Relevant to Teenagers.**

DEPTH FINDER

HOW THE BIBLE DESCRIBES SALVATION

To help you effectively guide your kids in this Core Christian Belief, use this overview as a launching point for a more in-depth study of salvation.

- **Grace.** No human being deserves eternal life with God. We all have sinned and can't possibly make ourselves good enough for God. That's where God's grace comes in. Grace is one element of God's unmerited favor. Only because of his grace toward us are any of us able to have relationship with him in any way. God, in his grace, has not only provided the way of salvation for us, but also strengthens us to continue following him (Romans 3:23-24; Romans 5:15-17; Ephesians 2:8-9; Titus 2:11-14; and 1 Peter 5:10-12).

- **Repentance.** To repent is more than to feel sorry about something. Repentance is making a conscious decision to turn away from sinful attitudes and actions and move toward a life guided by the Holy Spirit. True repentance results in a changed life. Repentance involves both human and divine action. When the Holy Spirit prompts us to turn from our sin, God wants us to respond in faith by embracing the grace he offers. True faith is impossible without repentance, and true repentance is impossible without faith (Matthew 4:17; Luke 24:46-47; Acts 2:38; Acts 3:19-21; Acts 20:21; and 2 Peter 3:9).

- **Faith.** More than simple belief in Jesus' existence, faith is trusting Jesus fully for both our present circumstances and our eternal destiny. It means believing and accepting his teachings as well as personally trusting in the miracle of his death and resurrection. When we place our faith in God, we make a conscious decision to believe and to act on that belief—but it is a decision we could not make unless the Holy Spirit prompted us to do so (Romans 4:4-5; Romans 10:17; Ephesians 2:8-9; Hebrews 11:6; and James 2:18-19).

- **Regeneration.** Related to the idea of being "born again," regeneration is the spiritual change in a human heart brought about by God's direct action. Through regeneration, our sinful spirit is reborn and made one with Christ. This change gives us the power to say no to sin. As Jesus came to life again after his crucifixion, we too have a new life in him. We become new creations, no longer slaves to sin, but free to serve God faithfully (John 1:12-13; John 3:3-8; 2 Corinthians 5:17; Ephesians 2:4-6; Titus 3:3-7; and 1 John 5:1).

- **Adoption.** In Roman law, an adopted child had all the benefits of his or her new adoptive family, but none of the debts or obligations of his or her natural family. In the same way, those who believe in Jesus are adopted as children of God and are freed from the debt of sin they owe. God adopts us as his children as an act of grace and love, giving us the privilege of becoming coheirs with Christ (John 1:12; Romans 8:5-17; Galatians 4:1-7; Ephesians 1:4-6; and 1 John 3:1-3).

● **Justification.** Because of what Jesus did in bearing our sins on the cross, God can declare us righteous before him. God's justice was satisfied at the cross because Jesus' death paid the penalty for our sins. Justification is more than forgiveness; it means erasing all record of the sin ever occurring (Romans 3:21-30; Romans 5:1-2, 6-11, 15-19; 2 Corinthians 5:21; Galatians 3:6-8; and Philippians 3:7-9).

● **Redemption.** Redemption refers to Christ's loving choice to pay our debt. The Greek word for "redeemed" was one that today might be stamped on a receipt, indicating "paid in full." The price for our sin was beyond our ability to pay. We were bound for eternal death because of the unpaid bill. But in taking our sins with him to death on the cross, Jesus paid our bill in full. Through faith in Jesus, we're freed from the debt of sin. Redemption also carries with it a "freed to" component. We're freed *from* sin and death *to* new life in Christ, as if we actually died with him and rose again as he did. So, Christ's redemptive act on the cross not only saves us from death, but continues to work in us daily, transforming us to be more like Jesus (Mark 10:45; Romans 6:4; Ephesians 1:7-8; Colossians 1:13-14; 1 Peter 1:17-21; and 1 Peter 3:18).

● **Sanctification.** "Sanctified" means "set apart." Thus sanctification is being set apart for God's service. It's the primary work of the Holy Spirit in the Christian's life. Some believe that sanctification is a one-time experience in which a person can receive complete sanctification in an instant. Others believe it's a process through which we gradually become more holy through spiritual growth over many years. Whichever is the case, sanctification involves an intimate communion between the Holy Spirit's work in our lives, and our faithful, obedient response to him (Romans 7:15-25; 1 Corinthians 6:9-11; 2 Corinthians 3:18; Philippians 2:12-13; and 2 Peter 1:3-9).

CORE CHRISTIAN BELIEF OVERVIEW

Here are the twenty-four Core Christian Belief categories that form the backbone of Core Belief Bible Study Series:

The Nature of God	Jesus Christ	The Holy Spirit
Humanity	Evil	Suffering
Creation	The Spiritual Realm	The Bible
Salvation	Spiritual Growth	Personal Character
God's Justice	Sin & Forgiveness	The Last Days
Love	The Church	Worship
Authority	Prayer	Family
Service	Relationships	Sharing Faith

Look for Group's Core Belief Bible Study Series books in these other Core Christian Beliefs!

about

Bible Study Series
for junior high/middle school

Think for a moment about your young people. When your students walk out of your youth program after they graduate from junior high or high school, what do you want them to know? What foundation do you want them to have so they can make wise choices?

You probably want them to know the essentials of the Christian faith. You want them to base everything they do on the foundational truths of Christianity. Are you meeting this goal?

If you have any doubt that your kids will walk into adulthood knowing and living by the tenets of the Christian faith, then you've picked up the right book. All the books in Group's Core Belief Bible Study Series encourage young people to discover the essentials of Christianity and to put those essentials into practice. Let us explain...

What Is Group's Core Belief Bible Study Series?

Group's Core Belief Bible Study Series is a biblically in-depth study series for junior high and senior high teenagers. This Bible study series utilizes four defining commitments to create each study. These "plumb lines" provide structure and continuity for every activity, study, project, and discussion. They are:

● **A Commitment to Biblical Depth**—Core Belief Bible Study Series is founded on the belief that kids not only *can* understand the deeper truths of the Bible but also *want* to understand them. Therefore, the activities and studies in this series strive to explain the "why" behind every truth we explore. That way, kids learn principles, not just rules.

● **A Commitment to Relevance**—Most kids aren't interested in abstract theories or doctrines about the universe. They want to know how to live successfully right now, today, in the heat of problems they can't ignore. Because of this, each study connects a real-life need with biblical principles that speak directly to that need. This study series finally bridges the gap between Bible truths and the real-world issues kids face.

● **A Commitment to Variety**—Today's young people have been raised in a sound bite world. They demand variety. For that reason, no two meetings in this study series are shaped exactly the same.

● **A Commitment to Active and Interactive Learning**—Active learning is learning by doing. Interactive learning simply takes active learning a step further by having kids teach each other what they've learned. It's a process that helps kids internalize and remember their discoveries.

For a more detailed description of these concepts, see the section titled "Why Active and Interactive Learning Works With Teenagers" beginning on page 57.

So how can you accomplish all this in a set of four easy-to-lead Bible studies? By weaving together various "power" elements to produce a fun experience that leaves kids challenged and encouraged.

Turn the page to take a look at some of the power elements used in this series.

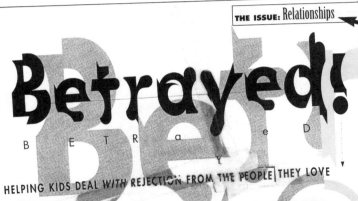

Betrayed!

HELPING KIDS DEAL WITH REJECTION FROM THE PEOPLE THEY LOVE

by Jennifer Carrell

THE POINT:

God is love.

■ Betrayal has very little shock value for this generation. It's as commonplace as compact discs and mosh pits. For many kids today, betrayal characterizes their parents' wedding vows. It's part of their curriculum at school; it defines the headlines and evening news. Betrayal is not only accepted—it's expected. ■ At the heart of such acceptance lies the belief that nothing is absolute. No vow, no law, no promise can be trusted. Relationships are betrayed at the earliest convenience. Repeatedly, kids see that something called "love" lasts just as long as it's ...rmanence. But deep inside, they hunger to see a

The Study
AT A GLANCE

SECTION	MINUTES	WHAT STUDENTS WILL DO	SUPPLIES
Discussion Starter	up to 5	JUMP-START—Identify some of the most common themes in today's movies.	Newsprint, marker
Investigation of Betrayal	12 to 15	REALITY CHECK—Form groups to compare anonymous, real-life stories of betrayal with experiences in their own lives.	"Profiles of Betrayal" handouts (p. 20), highlighter pens, newsprint, marker, tape
	3 to 5	WHO BETRAYED WHOM?—Guess the identities of the people profiled in the handouts.	Paper, tape, pen
Investigation of True Love	15 to 18	SOURCE WORK—Study and discuss God's definition of perfect love.	Bibles, newsprint, marker
	5 to 7	LOVE MESSAGES—Create unique ways to send a "message of love" to the victims of betrayal they've been studying.	Newsprint, markers, tape
Personal Application	10 to 15	SYMBOLIC LOVE—Give a partner a personal symbol of perfect love.	Paper lunch sack, pens, scissors, paper, catalogs

notes:

● **A Relevant Topic**—More than ever before, kids live in the now. What matters to them and what attracts their hearts is what's happening in their world at this moment. For this reason, every Core Belief Bible Study focuses on a particular hot topic that kids care about.

● **A Core Christian Belief**—Group's Core Belief Bible Study Series organizes the wealth of Christian truth and experience into twenty-four Core Christian Belief categories. These twenty-four headings act as umbrellas for a collection of detailed beliefs that define Christianity and set it apart from the world and every other religion. Each book in this series features one Core Christian Belief with lessons suited for junior high or senior high students.

"But," you ask, "won't my kids be bored talking about all these spiritual beliefs?" No way! As a youth leader, you know the value of using hot topics to connect with young people. Ultimately teenagers talk about issues because they're searching for meaning in their lives. They want to find the one equation that will make sense of all the confusing events happening around them. Each Core Belief Bible Study answers that need by connecting a hot topic with a powerful Christian principle. Kids walk away from the study with something more solid than just the shifting ebb and flow of their own opinions. They walk away with a deeper understanding of their Christian faith.

● **The Point**—This simple statement is designed to be the intersection between the Core Christian Belief and the hot topic. Everything in the study ultimately focuses on The Point so that kids study it and allow it time to sink into their hearts.

● **The Study at a Glance**—A quick look at this chart will tell you what kids will do, how long it will take them to do it, and what supplies you'll need to get it done.

● **The Bible Connection**—This is the power base of each study. Whether it's just one verse or several chapters, The Bible Connection provides the vital link between kids' minds and their hearts. The content of each Core Belief Bible Study reflects the belief that the true power of God—the power to expose, heal, and change kids' lives—is contained in his Word.

THE POINT OF *BETRAYED!*:

God is love.

THE BIBLE CONNECTION

1 JOHN 4:7-21	The Apostle John explains the nature and definition of perfect love.

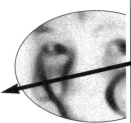

I n this study, kids will compare the imperfect love defined in real-life stories of betrayal to God's definition of perfect love.

By making this comparison, kids can discover that God is love and therefore incapable of betraying them. Then they'll be able to recognize the incredible opportunity God off relationship worthy of their absolute trust.

Explore the verses in The Bible Connection mation in the Depthfinder boxes throughout understanding of how these Scriptures conne

LEADER
TIP

THE STUDY

DISCUSSION STARTER ▼

Jump-Start (up to 5 minutes) As kids arrive, ask them to think common themes in movies, books, TV show have kids each contribute ideas for a mast two other kids in the room and sharing their f sider providing copies of People magazine to what's currently showing on television or at th their suggestions, write their respon es on new **come up with a lot of great idea** Even tho **ent, look through this list and ry to discov ments most of these theme have in comm**

After kids make several su gestions, mention responses are connected w th the idea of betray

● **Why do you think b trayal is such a co**

Betrayed! **17**

LEADER
TIP
for The Study
Because this topic can be so powerful and relevant to kids' lives, your group members may be tempted to get caught up in issues and lose sight of the deeper biblical principle found in The Point. Help your kids grasp The Point by guiding kids to focus on the biblical investi- gation and discussing how God's truth con- nects with reality in their lives.

DEPTHFINDER **UNDERSTANDING INTEGRITY**

Your students may not be entirely familiar with the meaning of integrity, espe- cially as it might apply to God's character in the Trinity. Use these definitions (taken from Webster's II New Riverside Dictionary) and other information to help you guide kids toward a better understanding of how God maintains integrity through the three expressions of the Trinity.

Integrity: 1. Firm adherence to a code or standard of values. 2. The state of being unimpaired. 3. The quality or condition of being undivided.

Synonyms for integrity include probity, completeness, wholeness, soundness, and perfection.

Our word "integrity" comes from the Latin word *integritas*, which means sound- ness. *Integritas* is also the root of the word "integer," which means "whole or com- plete," as in a "whole" number.

The Hebrew word that's often translated "integrity" (for example, in Psalm 25:21 [NIV]) is *tam*. It means whole, perfect, sincere, and honest.

CREATIVE GOD-EXPLORATION ▼

Top Hats (18 to 20 minutes) Form three groups, with each trio member from the previous activity going to a different group. Give each group Bibles, paper, and pens, and assign each group a different hat God wears: Father, Son, or Holy Spirit.

● **Depthfinder Boxes**— These informative sidelights located throughout each study add insight into a particular passage, word, historical fact, or Christian doctrine. Depthfinder boxes also provide insight into teen culture, adolescent development, current events, and philosophy.

● **Leader Tips**— These handy informa- tion boxes coach you through the study, offering helpful sug- gestions on everything from altering activities for different-sized groups to streamlining discussions to using effective discipline techniques.

holy **P**rofile**s**

Your assigned Bible passage describes how a particular person or group responded when confronted with God's holiness. Use the information in your passage to help your group discuss the questions below. Then use your flash- lights to teach the other two groups what you discover.

■ Based on your passage, what does holiness look like?

■ What does holiness sound like?

■ When people see God's holiness, how does it affect them?

■ How is this response to God's holiness like humility?

■ Based on your passage, how would you describe humility?

■ Why is humility an appropriate human response to God's holiness?

■ Based on what you see in your passage, do you think you are a humble person? Why or why not?

■ What's one way you could develop humility in your life this week?

● **Handouts**—Most Core Belief Bible Studies include photocopiable handouts to use with your group. Handouts might take the form of a fun game, a lively dis- cussion starter, or a challenging study page for kids to take home— anything to make your study more meaningful and effective.

The Last Word on Core Belief Bible Studies

Soon after you begin to use Group's Core Belief Bible Study Series, you'll see signs of real growth in your group members. Your kids will gain a deeper understanding of the Bible and of their own Christian faith. They'll see more clearly how a relationship with Jesus affects their daily lives. And they'll grow closer to God.

But that's not all. You'll also see kids grow closer to one another.

That's because this series is founded on the principle that Christian faith grows best in the context of relationship. Each study uses a variety of interactive pairs and small groups and always includes discussion questions that promote deeper relationships. The friendships kids will build through this study series will enable them to grow *together* toward a deeper relationship with God.

Parents Are People Too

BUILDING BETTER FAMILY RELATIONSHIPS

by Lisa Baba Lauffer

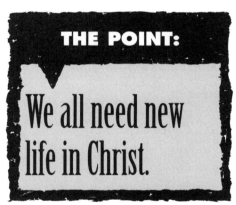

THE POINT:

We all need new life in Christ.

■ You might call it a war zone. Or, perhaps, survival training. But most recognize it as a family—with an adolescent attached. What is it about a student's junior high years that turns an otherwise sane, happy family into a batch of confused people trying to make it through the next six to eight years alive? Is it the growing independence? the young person's emerging personal opinions? the parents' grief over losing their child to adolescence and eventually to adulthood? Yes. While adjusting to changing roles and expectations, all family members experience frustration, anger, hurt, and sadness. These feelings quickly lead to a relational chasm bridged only by patience, love, and grace. This study invites kids to look at themselves and their parents in a new light—as imperfect humans who need the mercy of Jesus Christ.

The Study
AT A GLANCE

SECTION	MINUTES	WHAT STUDENTS WILL DO	SUPPLIES
Discussion Starter	10 to 15	BLOB ROLE-PLAY—Act out a family conflict in large groups with each large group representing a different member of the family.	Paper, pencils, box, twine
Family Evaluation	10 to 15	MODEL FAMILIES—Create models of their families and use the models to examine their family relationships, especially their parents.	Paper cups, markers, construction paper
Relational Bible Investigation	20 to 25	FAMILY MEETING—Hold a meeting to complete different tasks, including exploring Scriptures about everyone's need for a new life in Jesus Christ.	Bibles, "Family Meeting Agenda" handouts (pp. 22-23)
Closing Reflection	5 to 10	FILL MY CUP—Think of gifts they can give to each member of their families.	Paper, pencils, tape, cups from "Model Families" activity, construction paper

notes:

We all need new life in Christ.

THE BIBLE CONNECTION

ROMANS 3:21-26; 5:12-21; 6:5-14, 20-23 — These passages describe everyone's need for the new life Jesus can give.

I n this study, kids will creatively evaluate their relationships with their parents. Then they'll hold a "family meeting" to explore Scriptures about everyone's need for the life Jesus made possible through his death and resurrection.

By evaluating their families and exploring Scriptures, kids can adjust their views of themselves and their parents, seeing all family members as people who need new life in Christ.

Explore the verses in The Bible Connection, then examine the information in the Depthfinder boxes throughout the study to gain a deeper understanding of how these Scriptures connect with your young people.

THE STUDY

LEADER TIP for The Study

Parents and students can benefit from learning one another's perspectives about their families. Consider inviting your junior highers' parents to this meeting. Teach this study, revising the spoken text to address both students and parents. Adjust the activities according to the Leader Tips provided for including parents. And whenever groups discuss questions, encourage parents to answer those questions in reference to their relationships with their kids.

DISCUSSION STARTER ▼

Blob Role-Play (10 to 15 minutes)

Say: **Today we're going to explore our relationships with our parents. To start, let's do an unusual role-play.**

Hand slips of paper and pencils to your students. Say: **On your paper, write about a conflict a junior higher might have with his or her parents. You could write about a conflict you've had with your parents, a conflict a friend has had with his or her parents, or a conflict you make up. If you write about a real-life situation, change people's names to protect their privacy.**

Here are a few rules for writing your conflict situation: There must be four people involved. At least one of those people must be

LEADER TIP

for Blob Role-Play

If you've invited parents to your meeting, have them form groups with the students for this activity. Encourage parents to join groups that their own kids have *not* joined.

a junior higher, and at least one of those people must be the junior higher's parent. For example, you could write, "A junior high girl wants to go to a high school dance with her new high school boyfriend, but her mom and stepdad won't allow her to go."

Give students a minute to write their conflict situations. Then collect their slips of paper, and put them in a box.

Have students form four groups, and tie twine around each group. Say: **I'll randomly choose a conflict situation out of the box. Each group will represent a different character in the conflict I choose. As a group, you have to act out that part. For example, if I assign your group the junior high girl I described earlier, you have to decide how she'll react to her parents. Will she yell at them? Will she stomp out of the room? You'll have to figure it out as you role play. As you act the part together, think of how that's like relating with your parents.**

Pick one of the slips of paper out of the box, read the situation aloud, and assign a character to each group. Then have the groups role play. If you have time, you may want to do one or two more role-plays before moving to the discussion questions.

Then untie the groups, and have kids form foursomes to discuss these questions:

● **How was acting one character as a group like trying to get along with your parents? How was it different?**

● **How was being tied together like being in a family? How was it different?**

● **What's the most difficult thing about getting along with your parents? What's the easiest thing?**

Say: **Getting along with your parents is a challenge you face at this stage of your life. Today we'll discover how <u>we all need new life in Christ</u> and how that truth can help us through conflicts with our parents.**

LEADER TIP

for Model Families

If you've included parents in your meeting and have done the Blob Role-Play discussion starter, have the group form new foursomes. Have students form foursomes with other students, and parents form foursomes with other parents.

FAMILY EVALUATION ▼

Model Families (10 to 15 minutes) Set out paper cups, markers, and twelve-by-eighteen-inch construction paper. Say: **To begin exploring our relationships with our parents, let's create models of our families. Take a sheet of construction paper and as many cups as you have family members. Include everybody you consider as family: parents, brothers and sisters, stepparents, half brothers and sisters, and even pets if you'd like. Turn the cups upside down, then draw or write on each cup to indicate which cup represents which family member.**

When kids have finished, say: **I'm going to give you some directions for positioning your cups on the paper. Between instructions, I'll give you time to show your cups to your group and explain why you placed the cups where you did.**

DEPTHFINDER

UNDERSTANDING THE BIBLE

Young people's relationships with their parents affect their relationships with God. Some kids have good relationships with one or both parents, and these students can view God as good, loving, and forgiving. But many kids don't get along with their parents. Others live apart from Mom or Dad. Yet others have abusive parents, and when they hear the words "mother" or "father," they want to run away. Tragically, these earthly examples of parental authority taint kids' images of God, and young people from these families can't relate to God as the loving, forgiving, heavenly Father that he is.

If your students haven't had a good example to help them understand God, have them study this list of Bible passages to learn about some of God's fatherly characteristics.

- Psalm 103:6-14—God shows mercy toward his children.
- Proverbs 3:11-12; Hebrews 12:4-11—God disciplines his children in love.
- Isaiah 43:1-7—God is with his children through everything they experience.
- Jeremiah 3:19-22—God mourns when his children stray from him.
- Matthew 7:7-11—God wants to give good things to his children.
- Galatians 3:26-28—God shows no favoritism among his children.

LEADER TIP
for The Study

Because this topic can be so powerful and relevant to kids' lives, your group members may be tempted to get caught up in issues and lose sight of the deeper biblical principle found in The Point. Help your kids grasp The Point by guiding kids to focus on the biblical investigation and discussing how God's truth connects with reality in their lives.

Give the following directions, allowing a minute between each instruction for kids to move their cups and share their answers.

● **Move your cups to show which family members live under the same roof. For example, if you have more than one household in your family, you may draw a line on your paper to show which family members live in which household. If you or a sibling trade between households, you might want to place yourself or your sibling right on the line.**

● **Move your cups to show which family members have similar interests.**

● **Move your cups to show which family members spend the most time together.**

● **Move your cups to show how close each family member is to each other. For example, if you and your mother aren't close, you'd move your cup and your mother's cup apart—how far apart depends on how distant you feel from your mother.**

● **Move your cups to show what your family looks like when you're fighting with your parents.**

Say: **We all disagree with our parents sometimes. Let's explore some Bible verses that will help us view our parents differently, especially when we're arguing with them. Through our exploration, we'll discover how <u>we all need new life in Christ.</u>**

If you've invited parents to your meeting, consider having students do this Bible investigation with their own parents. If only a few parents attend the meeting, allow those parents to meet with their own kids. Have the rest of the students form groups with other students. Remind students and parents to respect each other's points of view.

RELATIONAL BIBLE INVESTIGATION ▼

Family Meeting (20 to 25 minutes) Before the study, make photocopies of the "Family Meeting Agenda" handout (pp. 22-23).

Give each group a copy of the handout. Say: **Hold a "family meeting" with your group by following the instructions on the handout. Allow groups to run their own family meetings, but circulate to answer any questions students may have.**

When groups have finished their meetings, ask:

● **How was working together in these meetings like trying to work things out with your parents? How was it different?**

● **What's one valuable thing you learned from the Bible passages that will help you get along better with your parents?**

Say: **As you discovered in your meetings, <u>we all need new life in Christ</u>. We and our parents make mistakes. We all need God's forgiveness, and we all need the gift of eternal life Jesus offered us when he died and rose from the dead.**

When it's hard to get along with your parents, remember that you need grace and your parents need it too. Allow your parents to make mistakes, and forgive them when they're wrong. Admit when you've made mistakes, and ask for forgiveness from God and your parents. These simple actions can bring you closer to God and to each other.

CLOSING REFLECTION ▼

If you've invited parents to your meeting, have students meet with their own parents for this closing reflection. Remind students and parents to listen and not judge the gifts they choose to give each other.

Fill My Cup (5 to 10 minutes) Set out slips of paper, pencils, and tape. Say: **To help our families learn that <u>we all need new life in Christ</u>, let's think of ways to encourage our families. Think of one gift you'd like to give each family member. These gifts don't have to be material things. They could be gifts such as praying for your dad, allowing your little sister to borrow something of yours, or helping your stepmom clean the house. On separate slips of paper, write down the gifts you'd like to give each family member. Then turn your cups right side up, and put the corresponding slip of paper into each person's cup.**

Include yourself, too. What gift would you give yourself? For example, you might promise to find something that reminds you of your new life in Christ, such as a leaf from a tree or a shiny new coin.

When everyone in your group has finished, explain your gift ideas to each other.

Before students leave, have them tape their cups to construction paper. Encourage students to take their creations home as reminders of the gifts they'll give their families.

You might have non-Christian students (and parents) in class who'd like to know more about Jesus' gift of eternal life. Be prepared to share the message of salvation and to answer any questions kids (and their parents) might have.

LEADER TIP for The Study

Whenever you tell groups to discuss a list of questions, write the questions on newsprint, and tape the newsprint to the wall so groups can answer the questions at their own pace.

DEPTHFINDER

UNDERSTANDING THESE KIDS' PARENTS

When you lead a group of junior highers, you need their parents on your side. Paying attention to what parents want for their kids will pay off as parents support you and your ministry.

According to Buddy Scott, family counselor and former youth worker, parents wish youth leaders would . . .

- plan events involving both teenagers and their parents.
- teach kids that their rebellious feelings are just part of their developmental process.
- help kids understand that parents are in their own developmental process.
- teach kids the importance of forgiving others.
- help kids learn to give, not just take.
- encourage kids to seek relationships with people who give, not just take.
- support the unique values of each family.
- accommodate kids with special needs, such as those suffering from physical disabilities, attention deficit disorder, or dyslexia.
- consistently and firmly address "kids who negatively influence the youth group."
- create Bible-learning activities that are fun.
- communicate messages countering the mainstream media's "wrong sexual messages."
- avoid judging their parenting abilities or perspectives.
- teach kids moral and spiritual truths without making kids think unchurched parents are bad.

(Adapted from "Thirteen Ways Parents Want You to Help Their Kids," Group Magazine, February 1993.)

Family Meeting Agenda

1. In your "family," read the following Bible passages: Romans 3:21-26; 5:12-21; and 6:5-14, 20-23.

2. Discuss these questions:

- What do each of these Bible passages say about who needs new life? about how to gain new life?

- How does knowing that we need new life affect your view of your parents? of yourself?

- Based on what you've learned, what's one way you could change your attitude or behavior toward your parents?

3. Do a "family chore" together. Agree on something nice to do for another group. For example, give back rubs to everyone in another group; or go outside, pick some flowers, and deliver the bouquet to another group.

Romans 3:21-26

But God has a way to make people right with him without the law, and he has now shown us that way which the law and the prophets told us about. God makes people right with himself through their faith in Jesus Christ. This is true for all who believe in Christ, because all people are the same: All have sinned and are not good enough for God's glory, and all need to be made right with God by his grace, which is a free gift. They need to be made free from sin through Jesus Christ. God gave him as a way to forgive sin through faith in the blood of Jesus' death. This showed that God always does what is right and fair, as in the past when he was patient and did not punish people for their sins. And God gave Jesus to show today that he does what is right. God did this so he could judge rightly and so he could make right any person who has faith in Jesus.

Romans 6:20-23 In the past you were slaves to sin, and goodness did not control you. You did evil things, and now you are ashamed of them. Those things only bring death. But now you are free from sin and have become slaves of God. This brings you a life that is only for God, and this gives you life forever. When people sin, they earn what sin pays—death. But God gives us a free gift—life forever in Christ Jesus our Lord.

4. Answer these questions:

● How did you feel when you did something nice for another group?

● How did doing something nice for another group affect how you related to the people in your group?

● How might you feel doing something nice for your parents? How might that affect your relationship with your parents?

● What's one positive thing you could do for your parents based on the Scripture passages we've read during this meeting?

● How can this group help you follow through on doing that positive thing?

5. Go on a "family vacation." Find a relaxing spot in or outside this room, and do the following:

● Pray for each other about your relationships with your parents. For example, pray that you'll get along better with your parents, that you'll follow through on doing something positive for your parents, or that you'll better understand your parents.

● Share at least one reason you're glad each person is a part of your group. For example, you could say, "I'm glad Stephen's in this group because he has good ideas for getting along with parents."

Stairways to Heaven?

THE MANY WAYS KIDS TRY TO REACH GOD

by Steve Saavedra

■ Your students belong to a "no free lunch" generation. According to Neil Howe and Bill Strauss, authors of *13th Gen*, today's young people believe in "personal determinism that requires each individual to take responsibility for his own condition...if you do bad and get caught, don't expect mercy." If you mess up, you deserve the consequences. But if you make the right moves, you can gain the world. It's all a matter of how badly you want it. In that context, how can your kids understand salvation? Eternal life isn't a prize to be won. This study helps kids understand that they can do nothing to earn their own way to heaven—nothing but accept the gift of eternal life that Jesus offers us all.

THE POINT:

Faith in Jesus is the only way to eternal life.

JERE SMITH

The Study
AT A GLANCE

SECTION	MINUTES	WHAT STUDENTS WILL DO	SUPPLIES
Stairway Creation	20 to 25	STEPS TOWARD HEAVEN—Create cardboard stairways that symbolize how people try to gain eternal life.	Cardboard, packing tape, scissors, paper, markers, index cards, pencils
Bible Investigation 1	5 to 10	DO AND DIE?—Explore the story of the rich young man in Mark 10:17-27.	Bibles, pencils, paper, tape
Object Lesson	up to 5	THE IMPERFECT CIRCLE—Attempt to draw a perfect circle.	Paper, pencils
Bible Investigation 2	10 to 15	FAITH WORKS—Explore Scripture passages about how to gain eternal life and use their stairways to express what they learn.	Bibles, paper, markers, tape
Reflection	up to 5	INTROSPECTION—Pray about how they try to gain eternal life.	Pencils, index cards from "Steps Toward Heaven" activity
	up to 5	STAIRWAY DEMOLITION—Demolish their stairways to symbolize the uselessness of trying to gain eternal life on their own.	Trash can

notes:

Faith in Jesus is the only way to eternal life.

THE BIBLE CONNECTION

| MARK 10:17-27 | Mark tells the story of the rich young man who asked Jesus how to gain eternal life. |
| JOHN 14:6; 17:1-3; EPHESIANS 2:4-9 | These passages explain that the only way to gain eternal life is through faith in Jesus Christ. |

In this study, kids will create stairways representing the ways they try to reach God and gain eternal life. They'll also explore the Bible story about the rich young man who asked Jesus how he could live forever.

Through this experience, kids can discover that they can only gain eternal life by believing in the life-giving power of Jesus' death and resurrection.

Explore the verses in The Bible Connection, then examine the information in the Depthfinder boxes throughout the study to gain a deeper understanding of how these Scriptures connect with your young people.

THE STUDY

STAIRWAY CREATION ▼

Steps Toward Heaven

(20 to 25 minutes)
Before the study, set out cardboard, packing tape, and scissors. When everyone has arrived, ask:
  ● **How many of you know someone who has passed away, such as a grandparent or friend?**

> **LEADER TIP**
> **for The Study**
> Whenever you tell groups to discuss a list of questions, write the questions on newsprint and tape the newsprint to the wall so groups can answer the questions at their own pace.

LEADER TIP for Steps Toward Heaven

Gather eight to ten cardboard boxes for every four students in your class. You can usually obtain free boxes from grocery stores, bookstores, or photocopy stores.

LEADER TIP for Steps Toward Heaven

Bill this activity as a contest! Tell groups that you'll judge their stairways on height, uniqueness, and decoration. (You can provide decorating materials such as crepe paper streamers, stickers, and brightly colored construction paper.) If possible, give an award to each group.

● **Where do you think those people are now? How do you know?**

Say: **Today we're going to explore how we can reach heaven and gain eternal life.** Have kids form groups of four. Say: **In your groups, build the tallest stairways you can using the materials I've provided. Remember that you're trying to reach heaven with your stairways.**

Have groups assign each member to a different task, such as designing the stairway, shaping the cardboard into stairs, and making sure everyone is participating.

After nine minutes, give groups a one-minute warning to put finishing touches on their stairways. When groups have finished, say: **As a group, sit in a circle at the bottom of your stairway. Tell the person on your right one way he or she was a good stairway builder. For example, you could say that someone creatively designed your stairway or was a good team worker.**

As the students affirm one another, give each group a stack of paper and a marker. Then say: **In your groups, brainstorm twelve ways teenagers try to get to heaven and write each way on a separate sheet of paper. Be specific and creative. For example, you might write, "giving to a beggar" or "praying seven times a day." Then tape your papers to your stairway, putting at least one sheet of paper on each step.**

When groups have finished, have groups present their stairways and explain their ideas for getting to heaven. Then have groups discuss the following questions:

● **How high would you need to build your stairway to reach heaven?**

● **How could you build your stairway that high?**

● **How was building your stairway like trying to gain eternal life?**

● **If you died today, would you go to heaven? Why or why not?**

Then hand each student an index card and a pencil. Say: **On the index card I gave you, write at least one way _you_ try to get to heaven. Then put the card in your pocket, your sock, or someplace else where no one else will see it. We'll use them later.**

☞ On our stairways, we've taped many ways that people try to get to heaven. During today's study, we'll learn that <u>faith in Jesus is the only way to eternal life</u>.

BIBLE INVESTIGATION 1 ▼

Do and Die? (5 to 10 minutes)
Say: **Let's explore a Bible story about a man who wanted to live forever. In your groups, read Mark 10:17-27. As you read, determine the ways the rich young man in the story tried to gain eternal life. Write each way you find on a separate sheet of paper. Then tape these papers to your stairways.**

When groups have finished, have them discuss these questions:

● **How does your stairway resemble the way the rich young**

Stairways to Heaven? 28

DEPTHFINDER — UNDERSTANDING THESE KIDS

We live in a post-Christian society. According to Rick Lawrence, editor of Group Magazine and author of the article "Reaching Kids in a Post-Christian Society," our culture today "has rejected God and taken his place on the throne." Throughout society, kids hear messages that they control their own destinies—if they make the right decisions, they can get whatever they want. When it comes to their eternal well-being, today's young people believe they can make the right moves and earn their way to heaven. If they've placed themselves on God's throne, they can place themselves in heaven, right?

But Jesus Christ clearly states in John 14:6 that faith in him is the only way to eternal life: "I am the way, and the truth, and the life. The only way to the Father is through me."

How do you reach today's kids, bent on determining their own fate, with the message of salvation? Lawrence suggests six strategies for communicating God's truth to today's young people.

1. Develop a peer ministry that encourages young people to tell others about Jesus Christ's gift of eternal life.

2. Use today's communication media such as drama and rap music to communicate the message of salvation.

3. Talk with conviction about your faith in Christ.

4. Be a consistent role model, communicating your message through your actions.

5. Increase kids' contact with adults by including parents and other adult volunteers in your ministry plan.

6. Create experiences that illustrate the message of salvation.

LEADER TIP for The Study

Because this topic is so powerful and relevant to kids' lives, your group members may get caught up in other issues and lose sight of the deeper biblical principle in The Point. Help your kids grasp The Point by guiding them to focus on the biblical investigation and discussing with them how God's truth connects with reality in their lives.

man tried to gain eternal life? How is it different?

● **How are the ways the rich young man tried to gain eternal life similar to the ways you try to gain eternal life? How are they different?**

● **How do you feel knowing that you can't earn eternal life?**

● **What does this passage say about how we can gain eternal life?**

Say: **Many people think that they can get to heaven by going to church, being nice to people, and by doing other good things. But the Bible says that <u>faith in Jesus is the only way to eternal life</u>. Let's do an experiment that will illustrate how we can't reach heaven any other way.**

OBJECT LESSON ▼

The Imperfect Circle (up to 5 minutes)
Give students paper and pencils. Say: **We're going to have a contest to see who can draw an absolutely perfect circle. But**

DEPTHFINDER

UNDERSTANDING THE BIBLE

The line between faith and works is thin, and discerning where it lies is a difficult task. The story of the rich young man in Mark 10:17-27 is an excellent example of this truth. The rich young man asks what he can do to gain eternal life, and Jesus tells him he should obey all the commands. When the young man states he has obeyed, Jesus has one more task for him to do. The young man must sell all he has and give the money to the poor. Unable to let go of his wealth and fully trust the Lord, the young man turns away.

Was this man condemned because he wouldn't do a work of charity? Or was there something more symbolic in his unwillingness to part with his wealth? The Disciple's Study Bible states that this story isn't about works gaining us eternal life but instead about expressing our faith through our works: "For this man a test of his faith was to do an act of mercy because Christ Himself commanded it and because the doing of it would substantiate any faith claim he might make."

James states, "Show me your faith without doing anything, and I will show you my faith by what I do" (James 2:18b). Help your kids see that when they accept Christ's gift of salvation, their natural response should be obedience. Help them maintain the perspective that their salvation is a precious gift and that their obedience to God is an appropriate response to that gift.

before we begin our contest, **all of you must spin around five times.** When everyone has finished spinning, say: **You may begin drawing now, but you must close your eyes while you draw your circle.**

When everyone has finished, have students show their circles to the rest of the class. Compare each circle with a circular object you have in the room, such as a roll of tape. Congratulate the person who came the closest to drawing a perfect circle. Then have kids form pairs to discuss these questions:

● **If you had to draw a perfect circle to gain eternal life, would you be able to do it? Why or why not?**

● **How is trying to draw a perfect circle like the way the rich young man in the Bible story tried to live forever? like the way Jesus said we could live forever?**

● **What's one thing you'll remember from this activity about gaining eternal life? Write your answer on your stairway, then share it with your group members.**

Say: **Drawing a circle while we're dizzy and have our eyes closed is impossible. It's like trying to get to heaven by doing the right things. Because God is perfect and holy, he can't be with anyone who is imperfect and unholy. So if we try to get to heaven through our actions, we have to do everything exactly right. Unfortunately, we can't. But because God loves us, he provides the way for us to get to heaven. <u>Faith in Jesus is the only way to eternal life</u>.**

BIBLE INVESTIGATION 2 ▼

Faith Works (10 to 15 minutes)
Have kids remain with or return to their stairway-building groups. Make sure each group still has a stack of paper and a marker.

Say: **Let's investigate some other Scripture passages about gaining eternal life by believing in Jesus Christ. In your groups read John 14:6; 17:1-3; and Ephesians 2:4-9. As you read these verses, think of this question: How can you reach God and gain eternal life? Write each answer you find on a separate sheet of paper. Then tape each sheet over one already on your stairway. Make sure you cover up all the old ways of trying to reach God and that you've written one new way for each member of your group. If necessary, make two or more copies of some of your answers.**

When groups have finished, have them discuss these questions:

● **Which stairway do you prefer—the "old" one or the one you've just created? Explain.**

● **Does your "new" stairway represent the ways you try to gain eternal life? Explain.**

● **What does it mean to you personally that Jesus is the only way to eternal life?**

● **Does this make you feel any differently about the people you know who've passed away? If so, how?**

● **What's one thing you can do this week in response to learning how you can live forever?**

Then say: **In your groups, use your stairway to creatively express what you've learned through your Bible investigations. You could sing a song, do a play, or recite a poem. Whatever you do, you must include your stairway. For example, one group member could recite a poem about trying to reach God through your own efforts as the rest of the group members try to blow a paper wad up the stairway.**

Give groups five minutes to create their presentations. Then have groups share their presentations with the rest of the class.

Say: **Through our Bible investigations today, we've found that <u>faith in Jesus is the only way to eternal life</u>. We cannot build a stairway to God through our own efforts, but God created and descended a stairway to us. When Jesus died and rose from the grave, he became our stairway to heaven. We can't reach heaven any other way than by believing in Jesus and giving our lives to him.**

REFLECTION ▼

Introspection (up to 5 minutes)
Say: **Let's think about what we've just learned today. As a group, remove from your stairways the sheets of paper describing the only way we get to heaven—through faith in Jesus. When you've removed them all, make sure each person in your**

group has at least one sheet of paper.

When students have finished, have them scatter around the room with each person finding his or her own space for reflecting. Then say: **Take out the index card you hid earlier. Compare what you wrote on your card with what's written on your sheet of paper. Are you trying to get to heaven by your own efforts, or are you depending on God and hoping in Jesus alone? Answer silently.**

After thirty seconds, say: **Today we've explored how we can't reach God through any efforts we make and how <u>faith in Jesus is the only way to eternal life</u>. What's your response to this truth?**

Close your eyes. In the next few minutes, I'll suggest some things for you to pray about. During this prayer time, please pray silently, following the suggestions that mean the most to you.

When students are ready, read the following prayer suggestions, allowing about thirty seconds between each one:

● **Thank God for the gift of eternal life. Thank God that we don't have to build our own stairways to heaven because he came down to us through Jesus Christ.**

● **If you feel ready to do this, ask God to forgive you for trying to reach him through your own efforts.**

● **If you feel ready, ask God to forgive you for your sins.**

● **If you wish, ask the Holy Spirit to help you depend only on Jesus for eternal life.**

Conclude the time of silent prayer by praying aloud: **Dear God, thank you for sending Jesus to earth so we can be with you in heaven forever. Amen.**

Distribute pencils to your students and say: **Look at your index card again. On the blank side of it, write your thoughts about whether you'll seek eternal life and if so, how. Write whatever you want because no one else will see it. As you write, remember that <u>faith in Jesus is the only way to eternal life</u>. Take your card with you today as a reminder to trust only in Jesus.**

DEPTH FINDER UNDERSTANDING THE BIBLE

When Jesus said, "I am the way, and the truth, and the life" (John 14:6), he used terms that implied his identity as the Messiah. He began his statement with "I Am," a term God used as his name in the Old Testament (see Exodus 3:14). By saying "I Am," Jesus clearly stated his position as God and alluded to his messianic role. The terms "way," "truth," and "life" are also messianic metaphors. According to the Disciple's Study Bible, "Jesus is the road to God, the accurate understanding of God, and our very existence come from God." Through Jesus we can travel the path toward eternal life, knowing the truth that he's the only way to heaven, and fully enjoying the eternal life that Jesus has made possible.

Stairway Demolition (up to 5 minutes)

Say: **Throughout our study today, our stairways have symbolized our own efforts at reaching God and gaining eternal life. Since <u>faith in Jesus is the only way to eternal life,</u> let's dismantle our stairways. This demolition will symbolize how we can't do anything to live forever but accept the gift God has offered us.**

If kids wish, allow them to take a piece of their stairways home as reminders that they cannot earn eternal life. Otherwise, have them throw the cardboard, tape, and paper into the trash can you've provided.

A Technicality in the Law

HELPING KIDS COMPREHEND GOD'S GRACE

by Amy Simpson

THE POINT:

Life is empty without Jesus.

■ Sports, school, music, TV, jobs, dates, youth group—today's teenagers have busy—and seemingly full—lives. Some of the activities are positive, some are negative. All of them, though, fail to fill the void many teenagers are trying so hard to satisfy. The things many young people pursue to provide them with peace and contentment just leave them feeling more empty. ■ Only Jesus can fill the void in the human heart. Today's teenagers desperately need to hear of the grace and fulfillment he extends to them. Teenagers need to learn that Jesus has paid the price for the wrong things they've done. Because Jesus has taken the penalty for their sin, teenagers who accept God's grace can have the peace with God they long for. Your kids need to know that life with Jesus is purposeful and complete. ■ This study provides an opportunity for teenagers to discover the grace of Jesus as it relates to salvation and to the everyday trials they face.

The Study
AT A GLANCE

SECTION	MINUTES	WHAT STUDENTS WILL DO	SUPPLIES
Setup	5 to 10	BRIEFING—Create balloon self-portraits and receive roles and instructions for investigating the guilt of humanity before God.	Bibles, balloons, paper, pencil, markers, "Role" handouts (pp. 43-46)
Investigative Experience	20 to 25	THE TRIAL—Investigate Scriptures and present evidence about the guilt of humanity before God.	Bibles, "Role" handouts, paper, pencils
	10 to 15	FINAL ARGUMENTS—Summarize their arguments and talk about judgment and grace as they pop their balloon self-portraits.	Bibles, paper, pencils, paper clips, balloons from the "Briefing" activity
Real-Life Application	10 to 15	COURT REPORTERS—Create pictures or words for display that represent everyday trials they face.	Blank overhead transparencies, markers, overhead projector

notes:

Life is empty without Jesus.

THE BIBLE CONNECTION

EXODUS 20:1-17; MATTHEW 22:34-40; JAMES 2:10	These passages describe God's laws for our behavior.
GENESIS 3:1-24; ROMANS 3:10-18, 23	These passages talk about our guilt and the sinful state we're in.
GENESIS 1:26-31; PSALM 139:13-16; ISAIAH 55:8-9	These passages talk about God's sovereignty in our lives.
JOHN 3:14-21; ROMANS 6:22-23; 8:1-6	These passages talk about the forgiveness and eternal life made possible through Jesus' sacrifice on our behalf.
EPHESIANS 2:8	This verse explains that we are saved by grace through faith.

I n this study, kids will adopt courtroom roles and hold a trial to determine the guilt of humanity before God. They'll have an opportunity to examine the role of God's grace in their everyday lives.

By investigating the position of sinful humanity before a holy God, kids can discover that the grace of Jesus can make them righteous before God and make their lives complete.

Explore the verses in The Bible Connection, then examine the information in the Depthfinder boxes throughout the study to gain a deeper understanding of how these Scriptures connect with your young people.

BEFORE THE STUDY

Photocopy and cut out the "Role" handouts (pp. 43-46). Make enough copies so that each person in class will have one handout and each handout will be given to roughly the same number of people. Fold and staple or tape each handout so that only the role at the top is showing.

On separate slips of paper, write "Ephesians 2:8." Put each slip inside a deflated balloon for each student in class.

THE STUDY

SETUP ▼

Briefing (5 to 10 minutes) As teenagers arrive, give each of them a balloon with the Bible verse inside it. Ask kids to blow up the balloons and tie them off, leaving the paper inside of their balloons. Set the markers in the middle of the room and say: **I'd like you to use your balloon and a marker to create a self-portrait. Draw something on your balloon that's representative of who you are. You can draw a face, a symbol, a scene—anything that represents *you*.**

When kids finish, say: **Today we're going to conduct a trial. Our defendant is humanity. Humanity is charged with breaking God's law and causing lives to be empty and sinful. Since you're a part of humanity, you're on trial too. Your balloon will serve as a reminder of that fact.** If you have extra chairs, have kids line the chairs up against a wall and put their balloons in the chairs. If you don't have extra chairs, have kids set their balloons against a wall for later use.

Have students form four groups: the Law, the Prosecution, the Defense Attorneys, and the Witnesses. Give each person a "Role" handout (pp. 43-46) according to the group he or she is a part of. Be sure to tell students to keep their handouts folded until you say it's OK to open them. Also make sure each group has at least one Bible. Then say: **Each one of you has been assigned to a group based on a role you'll play in the trial. You'll have ten minutes to read the handouts I've given you, gather your evidence, and formulate your cases. Then we'll hold the trial. Each group will have a chance to present its evidence, then respond to what other groups say. During the trial, we'll be examining how <u>life is empty without Jesus</u>.**

INVESTIGATIVE EXPERIENCE ▼

The Trial (20 to 25 minutes) Give each group paper and pencils. Give groups ten minutes to read the handouts, follow the directions, do the research, and prepare their cases. As groups work together, walk among them, offering encouragement and direction as needed. After ten minutes, say: **Court is now in session. I am your honorable judge presiding. Would the members of the Law please stand.**

When the members of the Law have stood, say to them: **You have three minutes to present your case. Please tell the court the position of the Law.**

DEPTHFINDER
UNDERSTANDING THESE KIDS

Helping teenagers understand God's grace may be a difficult task, but it's an important one. Teenagers are at a point in their lives when they are beginning to form identities, habits, and worldviews that they may carry with them for the rest of their lives.

In his book *Youth Evangelism*, David R. Veerman explains why it is crucial to help young people understand the grace of Jesus:

"Adolescence may be the first time a 'child' can make mature decisions. Because values are being tested and established, adolescence is the right time to introduce young people to Christ.

"The problem is that there is a great gap between the death of Christ for them and the modern teenager, between their lives and the Good News. People are needed to stand in this gap, to hold in one hand the hand of the Lord Jesus and in the other the hand of the young person for whom He died."

As a youth worker, you can stand in that gap. Young people, seeing the grace of Christ in your life, will want to know more. Demonstrate grace to your students— the ones God has called you to minister to. Many will respond and begin the journey of understanding God's grace.

To help the members of the Law present their group's position, ask the following questions as necessary:

- **What is the Law that God expects humanity to live up to?**
- **Do you have evidence to present to the court?**
- **Does the Law allow for any exceptions or loopholes?**
- **What does it take for someone to be labeled as a lawbreaker?**
- **What are the immediate and eternal consequences of breaking the Law?**

When the Law has finished presenting its case, say: **Thank you. Now we will hear from the Prosecution. Would the members of the Prosecution please stand.**

When the members of the Prosecution have stood, say to them: **You have three minutes to present your case. Please tell the court the position of the Prosecution.**

To help the Prosecution present their group's position, ask the following questions as necessary:

- **Has the defendant broken the Law?**
- **Do you have any evidence to present to the court?**
- **How has breaking the Law affected humanity?**
- **What is the punishment for breaking the Law?**
- **What do you think the defendant deserves?**

When the Prosecution has finished presenting its case, say: **Thank you. Now we will hear from the Defense Attorneys. Would the Defense Attorneys please stand.**

When the Defense Attorneys have stood, say to them: **You have three minutes to present your case. Please tell the court the position of the Defense Attorneys.**

To help the Defense Attorneys present their group's position, ask the following questions:

- **How does the defendant plead: guilty or not guilty?**
- **Do you have any evidence to present to the court?**
- **Is there anything the court should know about your client that hasn't already been pointed out?**
- **Do you think your client deserves what the Prosecution says?**

When the Defense has finished presenting its case, say: **Thank you. Now we will hear from the Witnesses. Would the Witnesses please stand.**

When the Witnesses have stood, say to them: **You have three minutes to present your case. Please tell the court the position of the Witnesses.**

To help the Witnesses present their group's position, ask the following questions:
- **Do you believe the defendant is guilty or not guilty?**
- **Do you have any evidence to present to the court?**
- **Do you believe the defendant should be punished? Why or why not?**
- **What do the defendant's actions, both good and bad, have to do with your testimony?**
- **How has grace affected humanity?**

When the Witnesses have finished presenting their case, say: **Thank you. You may take your seat. We've heard from the Law regarding the standards humanity is required to live up to. The Prosecution has told us what humanity has done wrong. The Defense Attorneys have stated their case as to why humanity should not be convicted. The Witnesses have shared their shocking information, proving that no matter how many good or bad things humanity does, <u>life is empty without Jesus</u>. Let's move on to the next phase of our trial.**

Final Arguments (10 to 15 minutes)

We'll now take a short recess while each group prepares its final arguments. During this time, prepare to give your final statements to win your case. Every group will have an opportunity to speak during the final arguments.

As kids prepare their final arguments, move from group to group, offering direction to kids who need help in preparing summaries of their viewpoints.

After a few minutes, ask:
- **Does anyone have any new information to share?**
- **Members of the Law, according to your evidence, what kind of life did God intend for humanity to have?**
- **Members of the Prosecution, according to your evidence, what is the cause of the emptiness of life for much of humanity?**
- **Defense Attorneys, what are some things that humanity uses to try to fill the emptiness of life?**
- **Witnesses, how does Jesus' grace remedy the emptiness of life? Does having a full life mean a person is always happy? Why or why not?**
- **Who believes the defendant is guilty as charged?**

● **Who believes the defendant should be punished?**
● **What punishment should the defendant receive?**

Give each student a paper clip. Ask kids to get their balloons and hold on to them. Then say: **We all deserve to be punished for our sin. We deserve eternal separation from God. To symbolize this, please pop your balloon with the end of your paper clip.** After kids have popped their balloons, ask:

● **Was it difficult to pop your balloon?**
● **How is this like the punishment we deserve for our sin? How is it different?**
● **Are the consequences of sin fair? Explain.**

Ask a volunteer to look up the Bible verse that is written on the paper in his or her balloon and read it aloud. Then ask:

● **According to Ephesians 2:8 and the information the Witnesses have shared with us, what is the factor that determines whether humanity is punished or set free?**
● **Do you think this is fair? Explain.**
● **What evidence have we uncovered that shows that <u>life</u>** 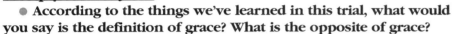 **<u>is empty without Jesus</u>?**
● **According to the things we've learned in this trial, what would you say is the definition of grace? What is the opposite of grace?**
● **How does knowing Jesus affect our present circumstances?**

Say: **Because <u>life is empty without Jesus</u>, it's important**  **for us to understand how the results of this trial apply to our everyday lives. Please take home your Bible verse as a reminder of the grace that's found in Jesus. Right now, we're going to take a look at how that grace can make our lives complete.**

LEADER TIP for Final Arguments

If you'd like to have refreshments during your meeting, the recess during the "Final Arguments" activity would be a perfect time.

REAL-LIFE APPLICATION ▼

Court Reporters (10 to 15 minutes) Give each person a blank overhead transparency and a marker. Say: **On this transparency, draw or write something that represents everyday trials you are experiencing. For example, you may choose to show how you feel "prosecuted" by standards and pressures, or you may want to show expectations and how you feel that you fail to live up to them. You'll have five minutes to create your transparencies. Then you'll present your pictures or words to each other. Please sign your name on your transparency.**

After five minutes, say: **As we look at the drawings or words you've created, think about ways God's grace can help you through these situations.** Ask each student to trade transparencies with someone else in the room. Have each student write one word on the transparency that symbolizes how God's grace is at work in the life of that person. For example, a student may write "joyful" on a transparency because God's joy is shown in that person's life. Then collect the transparencies and show each of them on an overhead projector. Allow students to describe or explain their pictures if they want to.

DEPTHFINDER — UNDERSTANDING THE BIBLE

In John 3:14, Jesus compares the Son of Man being lifted up to the snake being lifted up in the desert. This image comes from an account in Numbers 21:4-9. In this passage, the Israelites were traveling through the desert on their way to the Promised Land. As they traveled, they grew impatient and weary and began to complain about the conditions (as they often did).

Because of their complaining, God sent poisonous snakes. The snakes bit the people, and many Israelites died. This punishment drove the people to repentance. They came to Moses and confessed that they were wrong to complain against God.

When Moses prayed for the Israelites, God commanded him to make a bronze snake, mount it on a pole, and lift it up. If anyone was bitten by a snake, he or she could look at the bronze snake and be healed.

In *The 365 Day Devotional Commentary*, Lawrence O. Richards elaborates on this passage: "Even though the community is riddled with unbelief, there remains hope for individuals who are willing to trust God. Clearly, trust is an effective antidote for unbelief!

"Israel was learning that a purified people, willing to trust God, would enjoy victory rather than defeat.

"What a message for us to remember. No matter how flawed our past life, no matter how dark our present, we do have hope. We can determine now that the next steps we take on our pilgrimage will be steps of faith.

"We can believe. We can obey. And, when we do, we can win!"

When you have displayed the students' creations, ask:

● **What are some ways God's grace can help you through these everyday trials?**

● **When you're going through these trials, does life ever seem empty? How can Jesus fill that emptiness in your life?**

● **How can you respond to God's grace in these everyday situations?**

Say: **Life is empty without Jesus, but with his grace our lives can be full. Our choice to respond to his grace is a decision we must make every day and in every circumstance.**

Pray a prayer similar to this one: **Dear God, I pray that you will reveal yourself to all of us and make it clear to each one of us that your grace is at work in our lives. Please give us the courage to respond to your grace on a daily basis. As we realize how much you have done for us, teach us to accept your free gift and to live as your children. Amen.**

Role: The Law ||||||||||||

Instructions

1. **Do your research**. As the Law, you are responsible for looking up and pointing out the standards for human behavior. Use the "Evidence" section below to help you gather information by reading the Bible verses, discussing the questions that follow, and using your answers to strengthen your case.

2. **Prepare your presentation.** Be sure to assert yourselves, constantly making the point that the Law speaks for itself in the midst of arguments and excuses from the Defense Attorneys. Use the "Tips" section below to help you prepare an effective presentation.

Evidence

Exodus 20:1-17

• Why do you think God made these laws?

• Would a person have a fulfilled life if he or she kept all these laws? Why or why not?

Matthew 22:34-40

• Why do you think these two commands are the most important ones?

• How would the world be different if humanity always obeyed these two laws?

James 2:10

• Why does breaking one command make a person guilty of breaking all the commands?

Tips

• Be prepared to tell the court what God requires of humanity.
• Try to summarize some of the most important laws.
• Make it very clear that the Law allows for no exceptions.
• Explain the immediate and eternal consequences for breaking some or all of the laws.

Role: The Prosecution

Instructions

1. **Do your research.** As the Prosecution, you are responsible for presenting evidence that the defendant, humanity, has broken the Law. Use the "Evidence" section below to help you gather information by reading the Bible verses, discussing the questions that follow, and using your answers to strengthen your case.

2. **Prepare your presentation.** Be sure to point to the Law as the ultimate standard, constantly making the point that the evidence speaks for itself in the midst of arguments and excuses from the Defense Attorneys. Use the "Tips" section below to help you prepare an effective presentation.

Evidence
Genesis 3:1-24

- What effect did Adam and Eve's sin have on humanity?

- Why do we **all** have to pay for Adam and Eve's sin?

Romans 3:10-18, 23

- Who is guilty of being a lawbreaker?

- What are the immediate consequences of breaking God's law?

Matthew 5:21-24

- What does it take to break God's law?

- What are the eternal consequences of breaking God's law?

Tips

- Determine and point out the proper punishment for those who break the Law.
- Don't allow the Defense Attorneys to make excuses—if you break the Law, you're guilty.
- Remind the court that breaking one law is just as bad as breaking all the laws. Lawbreakers deserve punishment.
- Point out that because humanity is self-centered and disobedient to God, life has become empty and meaningless. This is not what God intended for humanity when he created Adam and Eve.

Role: The Defense Attorneys ||||||

Instructions

1. **Do your research.** As the Defense Attorneys, you are responsible for defending humanity against the accusations of the Prosecution. Use the "Evidence" section below to help you gather information by reading the Bible verses, discussing the questions, and using your answers to strengthen your case.

2. **Prepare your presentation.** Be sure to emphasize the positive things humanity has done, constantly making the point that it's not fair to concentrate only on the negative things. Use the "Tips" section below to help you prepare an effective presentation.

Evidence

Genesis 1:26-31

• How can people be lawbreakers if they're created in God's image?

• Are people basically good or basically bad? Explain.

Isaiah 55:8-9

• Is it possible to live up to God's standards?

• Does God really expect us to live up to his high standards?

Psalm 139:13-16

• Since God created us, doesn't he share the responsibility for our guilt?

• Can people be good without God?

Tips

• Point out that God's laws are impossible to keep—God doesn't really expect people to be able to live up to them.

• Remind the court that your client is good at heart. Give some examples of wonderful things humanity has done that you think outweigh the bad. For example, humanity has fed the hungry, created amazing inventions and artwork, and gone to church for thousands of years. Your client is even made in the image of God.

• Don't forget that God created humanity, so he should hold some responsibility for humanity's actions.

Role: The Witnesses

Instructions

1. **Do your research.** As the Witnesses, you are responsible for introducing new evidence that could clear or convict the defendant, humanity, who is accused of breaking the Law. Use the "Evidence" section below to help you gather information by reading the Bible verses, discussing the questions, and using your answers to strengthen your case.

2. **Prepare your presentation.** Be sure to point to the grace of Jesus, constantly making the point that regardless of the defendant's guilt, the punishment has already been taken by someone else. Use the "Tips" section below to help you prepare an effective presentation.

Evidence

John 3:14-21

● Why does belief in Jesus pardon people of their guilt? Is that fair?

Romans 6:22-23

● What can we do to earn pardon for our sins?

● Why did God give us the gift of eternal life?

Romans 8:1-6

● Does God's grace provide pardon for everyone's sins?

● What benefits come from accepting God's grace and following the Spirit?

Tips

● Point out that the punishment for humanity's sin has already been paid.
● Determine what the requirements are for a defendant to be found innocent.
● Remind the court that through God's grace people can receive pardon and escape the punishment they deserve for their sin.
● Tell everyone that Jesus' grace brings fullness to the meaningless lives of those who disobey God. Jesus is the remedy for the emptiness of life, no matter what the circumstances of humanity.

THE ISSUE: Faith

ROCK SOLID

rock solid

rock solid

by Siv M. Ricketts

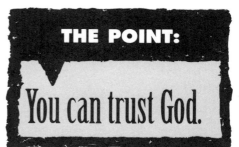

THE POINT:

You can trust God.

■ "How can I trust God if I can't trust the people I know?" ■Divorce, neglect, abuse, loneliness, adult responsibility, little to no opportunity. Today's junior high kids have little reason to trust anyone. They've been hurt so often by so many people that their walls of self-defense are almost impenetrable. They act tough and pretend that they're self-sufficient. They communicate that they don't need to be loved. But they do. ■ Your students need to know that even if they feel they can't trust anyone, they can trust God. He is the same yesterday, today and forever. He will never leave them nor forsake them. He can be trusted, and he loves them. ■ This study focuses on the reasons that junior high kids can trust God. It will help kids begin to take small steps of faith. They can see that God will always prove faithful. And once they begin, they'll find it's easier to trust him again and again.

"How can I trust God if I can't trust the people I know?"

The Study
AT A GLANCE

SECTION	MINUTES	WHAT STUDENTS WILL DO	SUPPLIES
Creative Opener	10 to 15	BABY STEPS—Indicate levels of trust by taking small or large steps.	Masking tape
Bible Exploration	12 to 15	WHO ARE YOU, GOD?—Compare God's attributes with human attributes and take small steps to the next activity.	Bibles, newsprint, markers, twine, scissors
	12 to 15	YOU WANT ME TO DO WHAT?—Rank situations in which it's hard for them to trust God and take larger steps to the next activity.	Bibles, markers, scissors, paper, pencils
	12 to 15	FAITH STEPS—Brainstorm a list of baby steps to begin trusting God and take steps to the next activity.	Bibles, markers, paper, pencils.
Application	up to 5	THE FINISH LINE—Demonstrate levels of trust by leaning against one another and recognizing trustworthiness in one another.	Bibles, marker

notes:

You can trust God.

THE BIBLE CONNECTION

LEVITICUS 11:45; 2 SAMUEL 22:2-3; PROVERBS 3:5-6; ACTS 17:24-25; 1 JOHN 4:7-10	These passages provide insights into God's character.
JUDGES 6:11-24, 33-40; 7:1-22	These passages describe the growth of Gideon's faith.
HEBREWS 11:1	This verse describes faith.

I n this study, kids will walk through Gideon's story and learn how he developed trust in God. They'll examine their own trust levels in God and others and investigate God's trustworthy character.

Through this exploration, kids can discover that God has impeccable character and that he is worthy of complete childlike trust and faith.

Explore the verses in The Bible Connection, then examine the information in the Depthfinder boxes throughout the study to gain a deeper understanding of how these Scriptures connect with your young people.

LEADER TIP for The Study

Whenever groups discuss a list of questions, write the questions on newsprint and tape the newsprint to the wall so groups can discuss the questions at their own pace.

BEFORE THE STUDY

Hang four sheets of newsprint to designate four stations around the room. Write one of the four following labels on each of the sheets: "Who Are You, God?" "You Want Me to Do What?" "Faith Steps," and "The Finish Line." Provide several Bibles and markers at each station.

THE STUDY

CREATIVE OPENER ▼

Baby Steps

(10 to 15 minutes)

Place a strip of masking tape along the floor in the center of the room to indicate a starting line, and ask students to stand side by side behind the line. Say: **I'm going to read a series of statements. After each statement, if you agree, take a small step forward. If you think the statement is false, take a giant step backward.**

Read the following statements and allow students to take the appropriate steps:

● **I think that people are generally trustworthy.**
● **I can trust my parents.**
● **I can trust my friends.**
● **I usually trust people, unless I have good reason not to.**
● **I think that people involved in organizations such as police or fire departments or churches are typically trustworthy.**
● **I can trust myself.**
● **I've never been hurt by someone breaking my trust.**
● **I think that other people trust me.**
● **I tend to believe people who say that I can trust them.**
● **I can trust God.**

Say: **Take a look at how far you've moved from your original position.** Then ask:

● **What does your current position tell you about yourself? Explain.**
● **Is it good to be a trusting person? Why or why not?**
● **What does it mean to trust someone?**
● **How do you decide whether or not to trust someone?**

Ask each student to find a partner. Say: **Share with your partner one time that someone broke your trust or a time when you broke someone else's trust. Then tell your partner about one person you think you can trust and why you trust him or her.**

When students have had time to share, say: **Many of us have been hurt so often that we've learned that it isn't safe to trust others. Having someone break your trust can be extremely painful. To protect ourselves from that pain, we build walls to keep others from finding out who we really are. We pretend to be tough, we laugh off put-downs, or we just don't admit that we might need someone to be vulnerable with. God understands the pain we've been through, and he promises that he loves us and wants the best for us. Even when you feel as if you can't trust anyone, <u>you can trust God.</u>**

DEPTHFINDER

UNDERSTANDING THE BIBLE

Our names are a very important part of who we are. They were selected for us by our parents, and they're the way we identify ourselves and others. Names may even play a part in shaping our character.

God has many names, and his character is revealed through them. The people learned to know God better and were able to trust him more as God revealed his names to them. Consider the following Scriptures.

● In Genesis 17:1, when God promises that Abraham will become "the father of many nations," God refers to himself as "God Almighty."

● In Exodus 3:14, when God tells Moses that he will lead the Israelites out of Egypt, God calls himself "I Am Who I Am."

● In Matthew 9:35-38 (New International Version), Jesus has compassion on the crowds and tells his disciples to pray to "the Lord of the harvest" for more workers to gather all the hurting people who need to know him.

● When the angel appears to Mary to tell her about Jesus' birth, he tells her to name the baby "Jesus." The angel says, "He will be great and will be called the Son of the Most High" (Luke 1:32).

● In John 10:11, Jesus calls himself "the good shepherd," who loves his sheep and gives his life for them.

● In John 15:5, Jesus says, "I am the vine, and you are the branches." We receive our life and produce spiritual fruit through our connection to him.

As your students commit to trusting God and following his will for their lives, they'll learn about him and be able to trust him more.

BIBLE EXPLORATION ▼

Who Are You, God? (12 to 15 minutes)

Pass out twine and scissors to kids. Have each student cut a piece of twine that is equal to the length of his or her arm from shoulder to finger. Then have each student cut a piece of twine that is equal to the length of his or her leg from hip to foot. Ask students to put the pieces of twine into their pockets for later use.

Have students form groups of four, then have them gather at the newsprint labeled "Who Are You, God?" Ask someone to read aloud Judges 6:11-24 while others follow along. Say: **You can trust God, but most people don't usually learn to trust him all at once. Gideon learned to trust God by taking baby steps of faith, and his first step was to be sure that he was talking to God.** Assign each group one of the following passages: Leviticus 11:45; 2 Samuel 22:2-3; Acts 17:24-25; and 1 John 4:7-10.

Say: **You have to know who God is in order to trust him. In your groups, read the passage, discuss what characteristics of God it describes, then come up with a statement that contrasts who God is with who humans are. For example, if God is trustworthy because he is strong, you might say that God's strength is a chain, but man's strength is a Slinky; or God's strength is a tree**

LEADER TIP for Bible Exploration

If your students aren't familiar with the story of Gideon, consider copying the Depthfinder (p. 55) about him, and distributing copies to your students before they begin the Bible Exploration activities.

LEADER TIP

for Bible Exploration

If the twine breaks while kids are walking from station to station, don't worry. Use the event to show how God wants us to break into a higher level of trust in him. To do this ask questions such as:

● How was breaking the twine while you walked like finding greater trust in God?

● How was it different?

DEPTH FINDER   UNDERSTANDING THE BIBLE

Hebrews 11:1 says that faith is the evidence of things we can't see. Christians have faith, but don't all Christians doubt sometimes? Sure they do. Peter doubted when he walked on the water, and Thomas doubted the reality of the resurrected Lord.

These are examples of believers who had doubts. The problems arise when people use their doubts as an excuse to not believe. They might say, "How do I know the Bible's true? I won't believe unless you can prove it to me!" or "I don't understand how a God who loves me can let me go through this, so I just can't believe in him."

Jesus is able to deal with our doubts. He pulled Peter out of the water when he doubted (Matthew 14:31). He held open his hands as Thomas touched the wounds (John 20:27). He had compassion on them both and told them to believe. As a believer, the best response to doubt is to pray about it. The father of a demon-possessed boy exclaimed to Jesus, "I do believe! Help me to believe more!" (Mark 9:24). That can be our prayer as well.

LEADER TIP

for Bible Exploration

To increase participation and enthusiasm, consider tying your own ankles with twine as you walk from station to station.

trunk, but man's strength is a twig. When you have your statement, send one person from your group to write it on the newsprint. Give groups about three minutes to read the passages and write their statements. Ask each group to explain what they discovered to the rest of the class. Then ask:

● **What would help you to have more trust in God?**

● **How can knowing more about who God is help you to trust him?**

● **What are some ways that you can learn more about God?**

Say: **One of the great things about God is that <u>you can trust God</u> with your life. He'll never let you down. And each time you exercise trust in him, it gets easier to trust him the next time.**

Ask the teenagers to use the smaller lengths of twine that they cut to tie their ankles together. Then say: **We're going to take small steps over to the next piece of newsprint. As you walk, try not to break the twine around your ankles.** Lead groups to the newsprint entitled "You Want Me to Do What?" Ask:

● **How are the steps you took over here like the first steps of faith Gideon was taking? How are they different?**

● **Was it difficult to walk that way?**

● **Is it difficult to trust God?**

Have students remove the twine from their ankles.

You Want Me to Do What? (12 to 15 minutes)

Distribute paper and pencils to the groups. Ask someone to read aloud Judges 6:33-40 while others follow along. Say: **Gideon began to trust God by doing what God asked of him, but before he went too far, he checked back with God to be sure that he'd heard correctly. With your group, brainstorm a list of five to seven situations where** it is hard for you to trust God. When you have your list, rank the situations in order, with "one" being the situation where it is hardest for you to trust God. Write your top three situations on the newsprint, and then pray together for strength so <u>you</u> <u>can trust God</u> in all areas of your lives. After groups have prayed together, have students tie their ankles together with their longer lengths of twine and step over to the newsprint entitled "Faith Steps." Ask students to try to keep the twine from falling off their ankles as they walk. Then ask:

LEADER TIP
for You Want Me to Do What?

Ask kids to tie the twine as close to the ends of the length as possible so they can take larger steps as they walk.

● **How is the twine around our ankles like our trust level in God? How is it different?**

● **What larger steps of faith did Gideon begin to take?**

● **Why do you think he took those steps of faith?**

● **Have you seen your trust in God grow or diminish over the last year? Explain.**

Have students remove the twine from their ankles.

Faith Steps (12 to 15 minutes)

Ask someone to read aloud Judges 7:1-8, while others follow along. Pass out a sheet of paper and a pencil to each group. Say: **Gideon had to take baby steps before he had enough faith to allow God to reduce his army to almost nothing compared to the size of the enemy's army. In your groups, brainstorm a list of baby steps you can take to begin to trust God more. You might want to use one of the situations you ranked at the last station, and brainstorm baby steps for it. For example, if you said that it's hardest to trust God with your family, you might choose to trust that God is working with them and try being patient with them while he works. When you've come up with five to eight baby steps, write one or two baby steps on the newsprint and share them with the rest of the class.**

After all the groups have shared, say: **Before moving to the next station, pair up with one person from your group and read Hebrews 11:1 together.** When students have read the verse, ask:

● **What does this verse tell us about faith?**

● **How are faith and trust similar?**

● **Why is it important for Christians to have faith?**

● **Is it easy or hard for you to have faith in God? Explain.**

DEPTH FINDER — UNDERSTANDING THE BIBLE

The Bible uses the words faith and trust somewhat interchangeably. But they never mean a simple belief in God; faith or trust must be followed by action. They require a life-response to Christ. James 2:14-19 explains that if you say you have faith but don't act on it, you really don't have faith at all. This doesn't mean that it's by our works that we're saved; we're saved by Christ alone (Ephesians. 2:8-9). But students need to understand that if they aren't willing to respond with their lives to Christ's death and resurrection, then they may not have faith in him.

● **What do you think you can do to make your faith stronger?**

Say: **Having faith in God isn't always easy, but without faith, we can't function as Christians. <u>You can trust God</u>, even if you have to start by taking baby steps. We've got one more station. Stay with your partner while we move over there to learn about the consequences of trusting God.**

Have kids move to the newsprint marked "The Finish Line" without tying their ankles. Ask:

● **Would you say your current trust in God is like walking with your ankles tied with the small twine, the large twine, or no twine at all?**

● **How does your trust in God compare to Gideon's trust in God? Explain.**

APPLICATION ▼

LEADER TIP for The Finish Line

You may want to try this activity with someone about your own size before beginning the lesson so that you can accurately explain how far the students can safely walk away from each other. In order to prevent accidents, stress the importance of being a trustworthy friend to the kids before you have them do this activity. Don't require students to participate if they're hesitant or uncomfortable.

The Finish Line (up to 5 minutes)

Have students assemble at the newsprint marked "The Finish Line." Ask someone to read aloud Judges 7:9-22 while others follow along. Say: **<u>You can trust God</u>, and he will watch over you. Because Gideon trusted God, God promised him victory even before the battle began. Now stand back to back with your partner, shoulders touching.** Allow students a moment to get in position. Say: **Slowly step away from your partner, keeping your shoulders touching, until you're leaning on each other for support. Stay in that position while I read Proverbs 3:5-6.**

Read the verses then ask:

● **Do you like being in the position? Why or why not?**

● **How is leaning on your partner like leaning on your own understanding? How is it different?**

● **How is leaning on your partner like trusting God? How is it different?**

● **What would happen if your partner didn't lean back on you?**

● **What do you think it means to trust with all your heart?**

● **What are some things you can do to trust God with all your heart?**

● **When should we trust others? When shouldn't we?**

Say: **God promises that when we trust him with all our hearts, he will give us success. Before you stand up straight, tell your partner one way that he or she is trustworthy. For example, you may say, "I know you're trustworthy because you don't gossip about others."** While students talk, write, <u>"You can trust God with all your heart!"</u> on the newsprint.

DEPTH FINDER

The story of Gideon is the story of a man learning to trust God by taking one step at a time.

Where It's Found	What Happens
Judges 6:11-24	The angel of the Lord comes to Gideon and tells him that Gideon will be the one to deliver Israel from its enemies. Gideon asks for proof that he is talking with God. He prepares meat, broth, and bread for the angel. The angel miraculously burns up the food, then disappears!
Judges 6:33-40	Gideon begins to do what God asks by gathering an army. Then Gideon asks again for proof that he is going in the right direction. He puts a piece of wool out at night, and asks God to send dew on the wool, but not on the ground. In the morning, the wool is soaked, the ground dry. The next night, he puts out more wool, and asks God to send dew on the ground but to keep the wool dry. In the morning, the ground is wet, the wool dry.
Judges 7:1-8	Gideon trusts God by obeying him and sending home anyone in his army who is afraid. Then God tells Gideon to take the rest of the men to the water and send home anyone who drinks by putting his face in the water. Again, Gideon obeys. Though he starts with 32,000 men, Gideon ends up with only 300!
Judges 7:9-22	Gideon and his servant steal into the enemy camp. Gideon overhears the explanation of a soldier's dream and is encouraged. Gideon dares to lead his small army to victory through miraculous means.

why ▼ Active and Interactive Learning works with teenagers

Let's Start With the Big Picture

Think back to a major life lesson you've learned.
Got it? Now answer these questions:
● Did you learn your lesson from something you read?
● Did you learn it from something you heard?
● Did you learn it from something you experienced?

If you're like 99 percent of your peers, you answered "yes" only to the third question—you learned your life lesson from something you experienced.

This simple test illustrates the most convincing reason for using active and interactive learning with young people: People learn best through experience. Or to put it even more simply, people learn by doing.

Learning by doing is what active learning is all about. No more sitting quietly in chairs and listening to a speaker expound theories about God—that's passive learning. Active learning gets kids out of their chairs and into the experience of life. With active learning, kids get to *do* what they're studying. They *feel* the effects of the principles you teach. They *learn* by experiencing truth firsthand.

Active learning works because it recognizes three basic learning needs and uses them in concert to enable young people to make discoveries on their own and to find practical life applications for the truths they believe.

So what are these three basic learning needs?
1. Teenagers need action.
2. Teenagers need to think.
3. Teenagers need to talk.

Read on to find out exactly how these needs will be met by using the active and interactive learning techniques in Group's Core Belief Bible Study Series in your youth group.

1. Teenagers Need Action

Aircraft pilots know well the difference between passive and active learning. Their passive learning comes through listening to flight instructors and reading flight-instruction books. Their active learning comes through actually flying an airplane or flight simulator. Books and lectures may be helpful, but pilots really learn to fly by manipulating a plane's controls themselves.

We can help young people learn in a similar way. Though we may engage students passively in some reading and listening to teachers, their understanding and application of God's Word will really take off through simulated and real-life experiences.

Forms of active learning include simulation games; role-plays; service projects; experiments; research projects; group pantomimes; mock trials; construction projects; purposeful games; field trips; and, of course, the most powerful form of active learning—real-life experiences.

We can more fully explain active learning by exploring four of its characteristics:

● **Active learning is an adventure.** Passive learning is almost always predictable. Students sit passively while the teacher or speaker follows a planned outline or script.

In active learning, kids may learn lessons the teacher never envisioned. Because the leader trusts students to help create the learning experience, learners may venture into unforeseen discoveries. And often the teacher learns as much as the students.

● **Active learning is fun and captivating.** What are we communicating when we say, "OK, the fun's over—time to talk about God"? What's the hidden message? That joy is separate from God? And that learning is separate from joy?

What a shame.

Active learning is not joyless. One seventh-grader we interviewed clearly remembered her best Sunday school lesson: "Jesus was the light, and we went into a dark room and shut off the lights. We had a candle, and we learned that Jesus is the light and the dark can't shut off the light." That's active learning. Deena enjoyed the lesson. She had fun. And she learned.

Active learning intrigues people. Whether they find a foot-washing experience captivating or maybe a bit uncomfortable, they learn. And they learn on a level deeper than any work sheet or teacher's lecture could ever reach.

● **Active learning involves everyone.** Here the difference between passive and active learning becomes abundantly clear. It's like the difference between watching a football game on television and actually playing in the game.

The "trust walk" provides a good example of involving everyone in active learning. Half of the group members put on blindfolds; the other half serve as guides. The "blind" people trust the guides to lead them through the building or outdoors. The guides prevent the blind people from falling down stairs or tripping over rocks. Everyone needs to participate to learn the inherent lessons of trust, faith, doubt, fear, confidence, and servanthood. Passive spectators of this experience would learn little, but participants learn a great deal.

● **Active learning is focused through debriefing.** Activity simply for activity's sake doesn't usually result in good learning. Debriefing—evaluating an experience by discussing it in pairs or small groups—helps focus the experience and draw out its meaning. Debriefing helps sort and order the information students gather during the experience. It helps learners relate the recently experienced activity to their lives.

The process of debriefing is best started immediately after an experience. We use a three-step process in debriefing: reflection, interpretation, and application.

Reflection—This first step asks the students, "How did you feel?" Active-learning experiences typically evoke an emotional reaction, so it's appropriate to begin debriefing at that level.

Some people ask, "What do feelings have to do with education?" Feelings have everything to do with education. Think back again to that time in your life when you learned a big lesson. In all likelihood, strong feelings accompanied that lesson. Our emotions tend to cement things into our memories.

When you're debriefing, use open-ended questions to probe feelings. Avoid questions that can be answered with a "yes" or "no." Let your learners know that there are no wrong answers to these "feeling" questions. Everyone's feelings are valid.

Interpretation—The next step in the debriefing process asks, "What does this mean to you? How is this experience like or unlike some other aspect of your life?" Now you're asking people to identify a message or principle from the experience.

You want your learners to discover the message for themselves. So instead of telling students your answers, take the time to ask questions that encourage self-discovery. Use Scripture and discussion in pairs or small groups to explore how the actions and effects of the activity might translate to their lives.

Alert! Some of your people may interpret wonderful messages that you never intended. That's not failure! That's the Holy Spirit at work. God allows us to catch different glimpses of his kingdom even when we all look through the same glass.

Application—The final debriefing step asks, "What will you do about it?" This step moves learning into action. Your young people have shared a common experience. They've discovered a principle. Now they must create something new with what they've just experienced and interpreted. They must integrate the message into their lives.

The application stage of debriefing calls for a decision. Ask your students how they'll change, how they'll grow, what they'll do as a result of your time together.

2. Teenagers Need to Think

Today's students have been trained not to think. They aren't dumber than previous generations. We've simply conditioned them not to use their heads.

You see, we've trained our kids to respond with the simplistic answers they think the teacher wants to hear. Fill-in-the-blank student workbooks and teachers who ask dead-end questions such as "What's the capital of Delaware?" have produced kids and adults who have learned not to think.

And it doesn't just happen in junior high or high school. Our children are schooled very early not to think. Teachers attempt to help kids read with nonsensical fill-in-the-blank drills, word scrambles, and missing-letter puzzles.

Helping teenagers think requires a paradigm shift in how we teach. We need to plan for and set aside time for higher-order thinking and be willing to reduce our time spent on lower-order parroting. Group's Core Belief Bible Study Series is designed to help you do just that.

Thinking classrooms look quite different from traditional classrooms. In most church environments, the teacher does most of the talking and hopes that knowledge will transmit from his or her brain to the students'. In thinking settings, the teacher coaches students to ponder, wonder, imagine, and problem-solve.

3. Teenagers Need to Talk

Everyone knows that the person who learns the most in any class is the teacher. Explaining a concept to someone else is usually more helpful to the explainer than to the listener. So why not let the students do more teaching? That's one of the chief benefits of letting kids do the talking. This process is called interactive learning.

What is interactive learning? Interactive learning occurs when students discuss and work cooperatively in pairs or small groups.

Interactive learning encourages learners to work together. It honors the fact that students can learn from one another, not just from the teacher. Students work together in pairs or small groups to accomplish shared goals. They build together, discuss together, and present together. They teach each other and learn from one another. Success as a group is celebrated. Positive interdependence promotes individual and group learning.

Interactive learning not only helps people learn but also helps learners feel better about themselves and get along better with others. It accomplishes these things more effectively than the independent or competitive methods.

Here's a selection of interactive learning techniques that are used in Group's Core Belief Bible Study Series. With any of these models, leaders may assign students to specific partners or small groups. This will maximize cooperation and learning by preventing all the "rowdies" from linking up. And it will allow for new friendships to form outside of established cliques.

Following any period of partner or small-group work, the leader may reconvene the entire class for large-group processing. During this time the teacher may ask for reports or discoveries from individuals or teams. This technique builds in accountability for the teacherless pairs and small groups.

Pair-Share—With this technique each student turns to a partner and responds to a question or problem from the teacher or leader. Every learner responds. There are no passive observers. The teacher may then ask people to share their partners' responses.

Study Partners—Most curricula and most teachers call for Scripture passages to be read to the whole class by one person. One reads; the others doze.

Why not relinquish some teacher control and let partners read and react with each other? They'll all be involved—and will learn more.

Learning Groups—Students work together in small groups to create a model, design artwork, or study a passage or story; then they discuss what they learned through the experience. Each person in the learning group may be assigned a specific role. Here are some examples:

Reader

Recorder (makes notes of key thoughts expressed during the reading or discussion)

Checker (makes sure everyone understands and agrees with answers arrived at by the group)

Encourager (urges silent members to share their thoughts)

When everyone has a specific responsibility, knows what it is, and contributes to a small group, much is accomplished and much is learned.

Summary Partners—One student reads a paragraph, then the partner summarizes the paragraph or interprets its meaning. Partners alternate roles with each paragraph.

The paraphrasing technique also works well in discussions. Anyone who wishes to share a thought must first paraphrase what the previous person said. This sharpens listening skills and demonstrates the power of feedback communication.

Jigsaw—Each person in a small group examines a different concept, Scripture, or part of an issue. Then each teaches the others in the group. Thus, all members teach, and all must learn the others' discoveries. This technique is called a jigsaw because individuals are responsible to their group for different pieces of the puzzle.

JIGSAW EXAMPLE

Here's an example of a jigsaw.

Assign four-person teams. Have teammates each number off from one to four. Have all the Ones go to one corner of the room, all the Twos to another corner, and so on.

Tell team members they're responsible for learning information in their numbered corners and then for teaching their team members when they return to their original teams.

Give the following assignments to various groups:

Ones: Read Psalm 22. Discuss and list the prophecies made about Jesus.

Twos: Read Isaiah 52:13–53:12. Discuss and list the prophecies made about Jesus.

Threes: Read Matthew 27:1-32. Discuss and list the things that happened to Jesus.

Fours: Read Matthew 27:33-66. Discuss and list the things that happened to Jesus.

After the corner groups meet and discuss, instruct all learners to return to their original teams and report what they've learned. Then have each team determine which prophecies about Jesus were fulfilled in the passages from Matthew.

Call on various individuals in each team to report one or two prophecies that were fulfilled.

You Can Do It Too!

All this information may sound revolutionary to you, but it's really not. God has been using active and interactive learning to teach his people for generations. Just look at Abraham and Isaac, Jacob and Esau, Moses and the Israelites, Ruth and Boaz. And then there's Jesus, who used active learning all the time!

Group's Core Belief Bible Study Series makes it easy for you to use active and interactive learning with your group. The active and interactive elements are automatically built in! Just follow the outlines, and watch as your kids grow through experience and positive interaction with others.

FOR DEEPER STUDY

For more information on incorporating active and interactive learning into your work with teenagers, check out these resources:

● *Why Nobody Learns Much of Anything at Church: And How to Fix It,* by Thom and Joani Schultz (Group Publishing) and
● *Do It! Active Learning in Youth Ministry,* by Thom and Joani Schultz (Group Publishing).

your evaluation of

Bible Study Series
for junior high/middle school

the truth about
BEING A CHRISTIAN

Group Publishing, Inc.
Attention: Core Belief Talk-back
P.O. Box 481
Loveland, CO 80539
Fax: (970) 669-1994

Please help us continue to provide innovative and useful resources for ministry. After you've led the studies in this volume, take a moment to fill out this evaluation; then mail or fax it to us at the address above. Thanks!

● ● ● ● ● ●

1. As a whole, this book has been (circle one)

not very helpful   very helpful
1   2   3   4   5   6   7   8   9   10

2. The best things about this book:

3. How this book could be improved:

4. What I will change because of this book:

5. Would you be interested in field-testing future Core Belief Bible Studies and giving us your feedback? If so, please complete the information below:

Name _____

Street address _____

City _____ State _____ Zip _____

Daytime telephone (____) _____ Date _____

THANKS!